Burt Rutan

Aircraft Designer

Other books in the Innovators series:

INNOVATORS

Burt Rutan

Aircraft Designer

KRIS HIRSCHMANN

KIDHAVEN PRESS

An imprint of Thomson Gale, a part of The Thomson Corporation

THOMSON

GALE

Detroit • New York • San Francisco • San Diego • New Haven, Conn. • Waterville, Maine • London • Munich

LIBRARY OF CONGRESS CATALOGING-IN-PUBLICATION DATA

Hirschmann, Kris, 1967–
  Burt Rutan: aircraft designer / by Kris Hirschmann.
    p. cm. — (Innovators)
  Includes bibliographical references and index.
  Contents: Fascinated by flight—Building a reputation—Imagination and innovation—To space . . . and beyond.
    ISBN 0-7377-3450-7 (hardcover : alk. paper)
    1. Rutan, Burt—Juvenile literature. 2. Aeronautical engineers—United States—Biography—Juvenile literature. I. Title. II. Series: Innovators (San Diego, Calif.)
  TL540.R875H57 2006
  629.130092—dc22
  [B]
                          2006006488

Printed in the United States of America

CONTENTS

An Aviation Pioneer

The field of **aviation** design is dominated by big companies such as Boeing and Lockheed. At these companies, huge teams of engineers labor over every detail of each model. A single engineer might work for months on a door, a wing, or a flap. When each element is finished, the parts are put together to make a whole airplane. The final result is professional, proven, and always airworthy. According to Elbert L. "Burt" Rutan, though, it is also unoriginal and even downright boring.

Rutan is an aviation designer known for dreaming up unusual aircraft designs and then building them. Other engineers have scoffed at some of these designs, but Rutan has shown again and again that even his oddest ideas work—and work well. Strangely shaped Rutan aircraft have flown around the world without refueling, blasted off into space, and accomplished many other amazing feats.

Over his 40-year career, Rutan has been the driving force behind hundreds of flight-related designs. In the early days,

Rutan brought most of his visions to life with his own two hands. Today the busy Rutan gets help from many skilled engineers. But the basic ideas are still his—and they are just as unusual as ever. In any group of aircraft, a Rutan design is sure to stand out.

By trusting his daring visions, Rutan has single-handedly changed the field of aviation design. In the process he has become one of the world's most respected **innovators**. He has received

Burt Rutan has been dreaming up and building new aircraft for 40 years.

many awards for his work, including the British Gold Medal for **Aeronautics** (1987), the *Design News* Engineer of the Year (1988), the Lindbergh Award (2000), *R&D* magazine's Innovator of the Year (2004), and *Inc.* magazine's **Entrepreneur** of the Year (2005). Four universities have given Rutan honorary degrees. He has appeared with presidents, on the news, and on TV talk shows, and he is a sought-after speaker for conventions all over the world.

Rutan may be famous, but he has not forgotten his roots. Flight is still his true love. Today he continues to dream up new ideas and put new projects into motion. As long as the ideas keep flowing, this creative genius will keep pushing the limits of aviation design.

CHAPTER 1

Fascinated by Flight

Rutan was born near Portland, Oregon, on June 17, 1943. His father, George, was a dentist. His mother, Irene, was a homemaker. The family already had two children: Dick, who was five years old when Burt was born, and sister Nell, the middle child.

Soon after Burt was born, the Rutan family moved to Dinuba, California. Burt spent the rest of his childhood and young adulthood in this small town just south of Fresno. It was here that Rutan and his siblings first fell in love with airplanes. This love was destined to shape the lives of all three children. Dick would eventually become a fighter pilot, and Nell would make a living as a flight attendant. Burt would become the world's greatest aviation designer.

Early Interest

The Rutan family's airplane fascination started when George earned a private pilot's license. He eventually teamed up with four other pilots to buy a small airplane that he flew on the weekends

Two museum visitors ponder the workings of an oddly shaped model airplane.

whenever the weather was nice. Sometimes the Rutan children tagged along. In this way, they were exposed to flight from the time they were very young.

Dick soon became interested in model planes. He bought, built, and flew many kit models—not always successfully. His models sometimes came crashing down to the ground. When they did, Burt was always there to pick up the pieces. By the time Burt was eight years old, he was using Dick's scraps to build model airplanes he dreamed up himself. "I didn't really build store-bought kits. I wasn't interested in the plastic models. I was interested in making things that fly and putting things together out of different materials,"[1] he remembers.

Young Burt knew nothing about aeronautics, of course, so there was no guarantee his homegrown designs would work. To test his creations, he convinced his mother to drive the family car down deserted highways at high speeds. Burt then stuck his models out the car's windows to see how they acted in a moving airstream. If it seemed as though the model would fly, Burt gave it a real-world test. His designs got better and better as Burt learned from his mistakes.

A Natural

Before long, Burt was entering his creations in model-airplane contests across the country. He competed in categories such as endurance, stunts, and free-flight-after-engine-shutoff. Usually he won. Winning did nothing to slow Burt down. As soon as he got back home with his trophies, he would retreat to his bedroom to design and build yet another model airplane.

By the time Burt was a teenager, he had years of experience designing airplanes. But he had never flown an actual aircraft.

A Goofy Kid

The Rutan family remembers Burt as a goofy kid with mismatched clothes and hair that stood up. This goofy kid, however, had unusual powers of concentration. "You'd see him looking out into space for minutes at a time, and if you asked him what he was doing, he'd say, 'I'm thinking,'" recalls Burt's father, George Rutan.

Burt kept to himself most of the time. "He never had any friends at school unless they built model airplanes," remembers George. "He never got acquainted. He's just sitting there in his room, he's not getting any air, he's building airplanes."

—Quoted in Alec Wilkinson, "Extraterrestrials," *Esquire*, June 1998, p. 87.

Rutan (right) examines a model of *Voyager*, the airplane he designed to fly around the world without refueling.

That changed in 1959, when Burt turned sixteen and began taking flying lessons. He immediately proved that he was a natural with real airplanes as well as models. He was a good pilot from the beginning, making his first solo flight after less than six hours of instruction. "I paid [the instructor] $2.50 an hour and the airplane was $4.50 an hour,"[2] he recalls. So for the bargain price of about $40, young Burt became a licensed pilot. It was the logical next step in a life devoted to all things airborne.

Learning the Trade

Burt graduated from high school in 1961 and headed off to California Polytechnic State University in San Luis Obispo, California. He studied **aeronautical engineering** and was a brilliant student. Burt's senior project won the national student paper competition of the American Institute of Aeronautics and Astronautics. He eventually graduated third in his class. Degree in hand, Burt was ready to look for his first real aviation job.

In 1965, when Rutan earned his degree, the world was focused on the space race between the United States and the Soviet Union. People thought it was more important to send a man to the moon than to study airplanes. So most aeronautical engineers were going into space-related jobs. Rutan resisted this path. Although he was fascinated by the idea of space travel, he did not particularly want to design rockets. "I was kind of being groomed to be a rocket guy . . . [but] I was among only one or two graduates who said, 'I'm going to focus on airplanes,'"[3] Rutan remembers. He thought there was a lot to learn about planes and their designs, and he was determined to do it.

Rutan did not want to join a big company, where he would have to work on details. Instead he looked for a job that would allow him to focus on whole airplanes. He took a position with the U.S. Air Force as a test-project engineer. Working out of Edwards Air Force Base near Mojave, California, he oversaw the test programs for fifteen different military airplanes between 1965 and 1972. The job was exciting and sometimes even dangerous. Flying in an F-4 fighter one time, remembers Rutan, "I was in a flat spin . . . and didn't have an accident, probably the only time that's happened. The next flight, which

Visitors examine an experimental supersonic airplane at Edwards Air Force Base, where Rutan worked from 1965 to 1972.

Rutan designed and built an all-wood airplane, the VariViggen, pictured here (lower right) with other aircraft.

was another spin test—I wasn't in it—the airplane did crash . . . I'd come back white as a sheet, feeling awful the rest of the day."[4]

Rutan's job taught him a lot about the way airplanes fly. It did not, however, give him a lot of design opportunities. So whenever Rutan got a spare moment, he worked on his own ideas. Between 1968 and 1972, he kept busy building an all-wood airplane that he called the VariViggen. Based on a Swedish military jet fighter, the VariViggen was Rutan's version of a personal military machine.

This 17-foot (5.2m) airplane had just one seat. With its main **delta wings** (wings that together form a triangle shape) and smaller wings on the nose, the VariViggen got people's attention wherever it flew.

Next Steps

After seven years, Rutan felt he had tested more than enough military airplanes. He left the air force in 1972 to become director of testing for Bede Aircraft in Newton, Kansas. This company was trying to develop airplane plans that could be sold to **home builders**, hobbyists who build their own working airplanes. Rutan's job was to polish the design of the BD-5J personal jet. Rutan did good work. However, Bede's publicity efforts were poor and the company struggled to find the proper engines for its planes. For these reasons, the BD-5J never became popular with home builders.

Rutan was frustrated by Bede's lack of support. He was also tired of working on other people's ideas instead of his own. After two years at Bede, Rutan decided that the only way to build the planes he imagined was to strike out on his own. So in 1974 he quit his job and headed back to the Mojave Desert, where he had started his career with the air force. At Mojave Airport, he found a small warehouse he could afford to rent and started Rutan Aircraft Factory (RAF).

Mojave was not the most pleasant place in the world. It was wind scoured, barren, hot, and remote. However, as Rutan points out, "The desert's a good place to fly from the standpoint of having clear skies, no clouds."[5] And flying airplanes was the main goal of RAF, so Rutan and a handful of employees settled into the desert lifestyle.

Early Lessons

When young Burt Rutan designed model airplanes, he learned lessons that would help him in his adult career. Here is what he says today about his early years:

> The airplanes I designed until I was 20 years old were airplanes that didn't carry people. . . . And because of that I could try the [darnedest] things. If they didn't fly, well, you learn more from a crash than you do from a successful flight. . . . You try to figure out why it crashed and look for limits of the envelope. Therefore, you learn both [airflow] and structural properties. To win the contests, I had the incentive to take risks. A designer working on airliners never learns that way.

—Quoted in Tim Stevens, "Just Plane Smart," *Industry Week*, December 15, 1997, p. 92.

Burt Rutan is pictured with an experimental remote-controlled airplane, the Raptor.

Rutan had no desire to produce airplanes for the general market. He just wanted to build the things he saw in his head. Rutan needed money to keep his company going, though, and he liked Bede's idea of selling airplane plans. He decided to come up with his own plans for **homebuilts**. By selling the blueprints to hobbyists, Rutan hoped he could earn enough cash to keep RAF afloat. It was an ambitious plan, and there was no guarantee it would work. But Rutan was consumed by his visions and dreams, and he was willing to take the chance.

CHAPTER 2

Building a Reputation

Money was tight in the early days of Rutan Aircraft Factory. The company could not afford a **wind tunnel**, a research tool that lets scientists see the way air travels around moving objects. So Rutan went back to his childhood testing methods. Residents of Mojave got used to seeing Rutan, with his unusual muttonchop sideburns, tearing down desert roads in an old Dodge Dart at speeds over 80 miles per hour (129kph). Airplane parts were always strapped to the car's roof. Rutan would see how the parts held up. Then he would take them back to the shop and change them to make them work better.

Wind testing and all the other things that went into designing and building an airplane took a lot of time. As RAF's key employee, Rutan did most of the work. He worked sixteen hours a day, seven days a week. It was a huge load— but it was worth it. Little by little, Rutan was seeing his dreams come to life.

Early Success

In 1976, RAF released its first set of plans to the homebuilt market. The plans showed hobbyists how to build a 14-foot (4.27m) airplane called the VariEze (pronounced "very easy"). With a top speed of 180 miles per hour (290kph), the little VariEze was fast and fun. It could carry two adults for about 700 miles (1,126km) when it had a full tank of fuel.

The VariEze was not just fun. It was also unique, because it was not made of metal like most airplanes. Instead, Rutan had found a way to layer foam and fiberglass to create the craft's body, wings, and other parts. This technique was called **composite construction**. The finished material was similar to a surfboard. It was light but very strong, and it was much easier to work with than metal. It was also much less expensive. Using Rutan's methods, a home builder could put together a VariEze in a few months for as little as $6,000.

Inexpensive and sleek, the VariEze was an instant success in the homebuilt market. But Rutan's low-budget design methods made some people wonder whether the aircraft was safe to fly. To answer this question, the U.S. National Aeronautics and Space Administration (NASA) bought a VariEze kit, built the plane, and tested it in an enormous wind tunnel. The VariEze performed well, earning high marks for **aerodynamics** and safety. These results made the aircraft even more popular, and VariEze plans soon flooded the homebuilt market. By the end of 1979, RAF had sold thousands of plans for the machine.

The next big step for RAF came in 1980, when the company's second airplane hit the market. The Rutan Long-EZ was an improved version of the VariEze. It had larger wings, a bigger cabin,

A full-scale model of the VariEze, a plane designed by Rutan, awaits testing in a wind tunnel.

and a more powerful engine. It could also hold more fuel. Fully loaded, a Long-EZ could fly for more than ten hours and up to 1,550 miles (2,500km). This long-distance flyer was just as big a hit as the VariEze had been. Between 1980 and 1985, RAF sold about 4,000 sets of Long-EZ plans.

The VariEze and the Long-EZ were by far RAF's most successful designs. But they were not the only Rutan airplanes that made it to the homebuilt market. RAF also marketed plans for the Solitaire (1982), the Defiant (1984), and a few other designs. Even an improved version of Rutan's first airplane, the Vari-Viggen, was sold in plan form.

The Canard

Their futuristic looks were one reason RAF's airplanes were so popular. Rutan loved to experiment with his designs, and he was not afraid to do things no one had ever tried before. As a result, RAF planes did not look like anything else on the market.

One feature that Rutan used again and again on his planes was a small set of nose-mounted wings called a **canard**. Rutan did not invent the canard. Some of the earliest airplanes, including one built by the famous Wright brothers, had nose wings. The feature had never become popular in aviation design—but Rutan was fascinated by it. He became even more interested after wind-tunnel tests proved that canards could keep airplanes from **stalling** (losing lift during flight). "I got real excited about having airplanes that would naturally limit stalls,"[6] he remembers. He started adding canards to all his designs.

At first Rutan got mixed reactions to his canard creations. Nose wings were not used very often on airplanes, and people

Burt Rutan Goes to the Movies

Three Rutan-designed aircraft have been featured in movies. The VariViggen appeared in the movie *Death Race 2000* (1975). The craft swooped down from the sky amid fiery explosions. The BD-5J, which Rutan designed for Bede Aircraft, appeared in the opening moments of the James Bond film *Octopussy* (1983). In the sequence, Bond escapes from enemy agents by flying the mini-jet through a hangar. And in the movie *Iron Eagles III* (1992), villains used a Rutan 151 ARES as a getaway vehicle.

Roger Moore starred in the film *Octopussy*, in which the BD-5J that Rutan designed was used for one scene.

Like many Rutan designs, the airplane known as the Catbird features nose-mounted wings called a canard.

thought they looked odd. It did not take long for pilots to realize that canards really worked, however. RAF planes were stable, stall-proof, and easy to fly. With so many benefits, canards were soon accepted across the aviation industry. They became one of Rutan's trademark design features. In the long run, they also had a major effect on the field of aviation design.

Just for Fun

The canard was one of Rutan's most visible innovations, but it was far from the only one. Rutan never seemed to run out of new and original design ideas. At home, in restaurants, and on the road he sketched rough plans onto napkins or any scraps of paper he could find. Rutan stuck these sketches into his pocket. Then he copied the most promising ones into a special design notebook. The notebook soon held hundreds of ideas.

The biggest joy in Rutan's life was turning his sketches into reality. He never saw designing and building airplanes as work. He saw it as fun, and he did his best to pass this attitude on to his employees. He encouraged the people who worked at RAF to be original and to enjoy their jobs. "Fun is absolutely, positively the most productive thing a development company can have," he says today. "If you continue to have fun in your business, you will have success in your business."[7] Rutan himself loved his job so much that he started calling his factory "the candy store." The airplanes were the candy. Rutan and his employees were the excited kids grinning at the sweet treats that surrounded them.

To Rutan, having fun did not mean doing the same old things in the same old way. It meant taking risks, and sometimes that meant failing.

I force myself not to manage everything, even when I can see that a . . . young engineer is going to [mess] it up. It's better to let him make the mistake and learn from it. The guy who's most creative is the guy who's making the most mistakes. He's probably the guy who had the courage to try several new things. If you fire him, everybody else around him is certainly not going to take risks. [And] once you stop taking risks, you're doomed in the long run. [8]

A New Market

Rutan's way of working got results. RAF kept churning out groundbreaking designs—and Rutan kept getting noticed. By the

early 1980s, Rutan's name was well known in aviation circles. People saw him as a problem solver. As a result, big companies started coming to Rutan for advice on tricky design issues.

It did not take long for the trickle of phone calls to turn into a steady flow. To meet this new demand, Rutan started a second company in 1982. The company was called Scaled Composites, LLC (or Scaled for short). Rutan did not want to produce commercial aircraft through Scaled. Instead, he wanted to be an adviser to the U.S. government and private industries. Scaled's purpose was to design and test custom airplanes for these clients. To test a design, Scaled employees would build a **prototype**—

This prototype of a jet known as Vantage is one of many produced at Rutan's company, Scaled Composites.

Creative Genius

In big companies, designers are expected to come up with creative designs while staring at computer screens. According to Rutan, this approach seldom works. "Fresh ideas rarely come out of what you consider a normal environment," he explains. To escape this trap, Rutan often heads to remote areas when he wants to get creative. On one brainstorming trip, Rutan and a designer friend traveled to Hawaii. "We found a deserted beach and brought sketch pads—no calculators. We sat and tried to envision how to build tomorrow's light plane," Rutan recalls. By the time Rutan returned to Mojave, he had a notebook full of sketches and dozens of new ideas to pursue.

—Quoted in Jim Schefter, "Wild Wings Reshape the Way We Fly," *Popular Science*, February 1990, p. 61.

Rutan (second from right) consults with his colleagues on the building of a new airplane.

a smaller-than-full-size, working model. Flying the models let workers find and fix design bugs before an airplane went into full production.

Scaled got its first big job right away, when the company was hired to design and test a business airplane called Starship for Beech Aircraft Corporation. The first full-size Starship flew in 1986, and the airplane went into production in 1988. Other projects followed, and Rutan's reputation grew. Soon the designer was giving advice to NASA and other clients around the world. Already a star in the hobby business, Rutan was now becoming known in commercial aviation as well.

CHAPTER 3

Imagination and Innovation

B y the mid-1980s, Rutan was becoming frustrated with his homebuilt aircraft business. Sales were still good, but RAF was starting to have legal troubles. People who ran into trouble with RAF's aircraft were suing the company. There was nothing wrong with Rutan's designs, but flight is risky and accidents happen. Rutan was forced to spend hundreds of thousands of dollars to defend himself from a few angry customers.

During this same period, Scaled was enjoying huge success. Keeping on top of the company's workload was a full-time job for Rutan. Scaled was also fun, unlike RAF, which was now a headache instead of a pleasure. So in 1985, Rutan decided to phase out his homebuilt business and focus on Scaled. RAF would stay open to help people who owned or were currently building Rutan aircraft, but it would not design or sell any new planes.

This decision disappointed Rutan's homebuilt customers, but it did nothing to harm his reputation in the commercial world.

Known everywhere by now as an aviation expert, Rutan got to work on Scaled's many assignments.

Decades of Invention

Over the next two decades, Rutan revolutionized the field of aviation—and a few other industries as well. One of Scaled's early projects was a 108-foot (33m) sail for the *Stars & Stripes,* a

A Scaled Composites technician assembles the fuselage of a small jet airplane.

world-class racing yacht. The sail was shaped like an enormous airplane wing. Using this sail, the *Stars & Stripes* breezed to victory in the 1988 America's Cup race.

Another interesting Scaled product was an ultralight show car for General Motors. Produced in 1992, this car was made of composite materials instead of metal. Typical passenger vehicles weigh about 3,500 pounds (1,590kg). Rutan's creation weighed only 420 pounds (191kg).

With sails, cars, and other inventions to his name, Rutan was proving that he could design just about anything. Still, he was most interested in aviation design. Over the years, Scaled turned out dozens of airplanes and flight-related products for a wide variety of clients. In 1989, for instance, the company built and tested a model of the B-2 "stealth" bomber for the U.S. Air Force. In 1996, the company released an aircraft called Boomerang that looked like it would never fly but that was unusually stable in the air. And in 1998, Scaled designed and built a high-**altitude** aircraft called Proteus. This vehicle was meant to be used for scouting missions, research, space launches, and other high-altitude needs. In October 2000, Proteus set an altitude record of 62,786 feet (19,137m)—the greatest height ever reached by a vehicle of its weight.

These aircraft are just a few examples of Scaled's work. From 1985 onward, original designs poured out of the factory in a steady stream. With names like Pond Racer, Catbird, Eagle Eye, Raptor, and Triumph, Rutan aircraft were always eye-catching and exciting.

Flight of *Voyager*

One of Burt Rutan's most famous designs was one of his earliest ones. The idea for the record-breaking airplane came in 1981.

Boomerang, an airplane designed by Rutan, proved unusually stable in flight.

Hard to Fly

Rutan remembers that *Voyager* was very hard to fly. In fact, he recalls, "Our data showed that the flight was improbable. . . . If we had been working for NASA or Boeing, they would never have let us leave the ground. The wings flapped like a bird. The airplane itself was too frail to land anywhere except on a runway, [but] most of the flight was over water. If you had to put it down, you die."

Dick Rutan later said that his brother was more concerned about his airplanes than he was about his pilots. He remembers, for instance, that Burt did not want to put radar into *Voyager* because he thought it was too heavy. Dick argued with his brother until Burt finally agreed to add this important piece of safety equipment.

—Quoted in Alec Wilkinson, "Extraterrestrials," *Esquire,* June 1998, p. 90.

Despite damage to its wing (pictured), *Voyager* **completed a round-the-world nonstop flight without refueling.**

Burt, his brother Dick, and Dick's girlfriend, Jeana Yeager, were having lunch in a Mojave restaurant and coming up with new concepts, as usual. At some point Burt turned to Dick and said, "Why don't you fly around the world? I think it can be done."[9] Burt was referring to an around-the-world flight without stopping or refueling. No one had been able to conquer this aviation milestone, but Burt thought he could design the right airplane for the job.

This conversation kicked off Rutan's biggest project yet. The globe-circling airplane, which was eventually named *Voyager*, took two years to build and two more years to test. The finished craft had a small cigar-shaped cabin. To either side of the cabin were stabilizing bars, known as booms, that also contained fuel tanks. *Voyager*'s extremely slim wings stretched about 110 feet (33.5m) from tip to tip. When empty, the craft weighed just 939 pounds (425kg).

Tricky Flying

Flying *Voyager* was tricky, but copilots Dick and Jeana were determined to complete their mission. They took off from Edwards Air Force Base just after 8:00 A.M. on December 14, 1986. The historic flight that followed was exhausting and emotional. Sometimes it was even dangerous. On the second day of the flight, *Voyager* had to dodge a hurricane. The aircraft nearly hit a mountain when it flew over Africa, and its engine failed at one point. Luckily the pilots managed to restart the engine before *Voyager* lost enough speed to fall from the sky.

Although the flight was difficult, it was successful. On the morning of December 23, *Voyager* returned to its starting point. It touched down at 8:05 A.M.—9 days, 3 minutes, and 44 seconds after takeoff. The little airplane had traveled an incredible 24,986 miles (42,212km) at an average speed of 116 miles per hour (186kph). By doing so, it had earned a spot in the record books and in aviation history as well. Today *Voyager* hangs in the Smithsonian National Air and Space Museum in Washington, D.C., where it is seen by millions of visitors each year.

Around the World Again

In 1999 the subject of around-the-world flight came up again. Dick Rutan told a pilot named Steve Fossett that he should try to fly around the world, without stopping, by himself. He also told Fossett that he thought his brother Burt could design the

right airplane to accomplish this feat. Fossett was intrigued. He got in touch with Burt, and soon the *GlobalFlyer* project was born. (The aircraft was later renamed the *Virgin Atlantic Global-Flyer* when Virgin Atlantic Airways contributed money to the project.)

The aircraft Rutan dreamed up for Fossett was similar to *Voyager* in many ways. *GlobalFlyer* had the same slender cabin, fuel booms, and wings. With a width of 114 feet (34.7m), it was also about the same size as *Voyager.* The airplane did, however, have some new features, including a powerful jet engine rather than propellers. Using this engine, *GlobalFlyer* could reach a top speed of 275 miles per hour (442kph). Traveling more quickly

Burt Rutan designed *GlobalFlyer* (pictured) for pilot Steve Fossett, who wanted to fly solo around the world without stopping or refueling.

would cut down the aircraft's around-the-world time—an important feature for a solo pilot. In addition, *GlobalFlyer* was designed to fly at altitudes of up to 50,000 feet (15,240m). By keeping the airplane high in the sky, Rutan hoped to avoid bad weather and make the flight safer.

After years of testing, *GlobalFlyer* was ready to attempt an around-the-world flight. On February 28, 2005, the craft took off from an airport in Salina, Kansas. Fossett was at the controls. Heavy with fuel, the aircraft had to taxi for 2 miles (3.2km) before it was moving fast enough to get off the ground. Once in the air, however, the *GlobalFlyer* flew beautifully. It made its way around the world and returned to Salina on March 3. The flight took 2 days, 19 hours, 1 minute, and 46 seconds, and it covered a distance of 22,882 miles (36,817km). It was another proud moment for aviation—and another record for Rutan.

The *GlobalFlyer* shattered yet another record in February 2006. Flown once again by Fossett, the aircraft stayed aloft for 3 days, 4 hours, and 45 minutes without refueling. The total distance flown was 26,398 miles (42,469km), a new world record for the longest flight by any type of aircraft.

A Lasting Impression

The *Voyager* and *GlobalFlyer* stories were widely publicized. The airplanes and their incredible journeys got most of the attention, but Rutan got plenty of publicity as well. After *Voyager's* flight, for instance, Rutan was photographed shaking hands with U.S. president Ronald Reagan. He was quoted in popular magazines and newspapers, from *Time* to *National Geographic* to *USA Today*, and

Voyager pilots Jeana Yeager and Dick Rutan wave to well-wishers after completing their historic flight.

he received awards from all sorts of scientific organizations. Already well known in aviation circles, Rutan was suddenly a household name around the world.

Success changed Rutan's role at Scaled Composites. The designer got busier and busier as the company's workload increased. Rutan still came up with most of the ideas, but he had much less time to do the actual work. During normal business hours, said the designer in a 2002 interview, "I do marketing. I do proposals. I host prospective customers . . . and see if we can structure a program around them."[10]

A Famous Crash

On October 12, 1997, a famous musician named John Denver died after crashing a Rutan Long-EZ into the ocean off the California coast. According to the accident report, the Long-EZ had not been built according to Rutan's original plans. Some switches were installed in awkward places, and some gauges were not clearly marked. These changes probably confused Denver and ultimately cost him his life.

Rescue workers carry the body of singer John Denver, who died in the crash of a plane built from modified Rutan plans.

No matter how busy Rutan got, though, he always found time for a little hands-on involvement. "I also get in and work on building airplanes. I get my hands dirty, still. . . . The general rule here is that you don't get the privilege of designing something unless you have the capability of building it with your own hands,"[11] he says. By doing some of the work himself, Rutan makes sure his skills stay sharp. He also ensures that each Scaled aircraft meets his high standards. Rutan is not afraid to fail during the design process—but when it comes to finished aircraft, perfection is the only result that counts.

CHAPTER 4

To Space . . . and Beyond

Rutan has spent most of his career designing airplanes. In recent years, however, he has become more interested in space travel. With his wildly original creations, Rutan is shaking up the field of space aviation just as he has done with regular aviation for so long.

Those who know Rutan do not find it surprising that the designer skipped the frantic space-race years of the 1960s, only to plunge into space design decades later. Major space agencies today do not seem to be as original and exciting as they used to be. Creativity is desperately needed, and it is only natural that an innovator like Rutan would become interested.

Early Inspiration

Rutan credits his interest in space to an old television show. In 1955, a Walt Disney series called *Disneyland* aired two episodes about space travel. The first episode, "Man in Space," looked at the future of manned space travel. The second episode, "Man and the

Moon," talked about the possibility of sending people to the moon. The shows featured German rocket genius Wernher von Braun, who later helped design the first spacecraft to take humans to the moon and back.

Rutan, who was only twelve years old at the time, was dazzled by the series. "It influenced my life like you wouldn't believe," he says today. Young Burt dreamed of going into space, just like the fictional TV astronauts. Those dreams got even more exciting when humans actually did start traveling into space and

The appearance of rocket scientist Wernher von Braun on a television show in 1955 caused Burt Rutan to dream of traveling into outer space.

Microsoft cofounder Paul Allen (right) and Burt Rutan (left) set out to design and build the first craft to fly into space without the backing of any government.

back. "We're sitting there amazed throughout the 1960s . . . because our country was going from Walt Disney and von Braun talking about it . . . all the way to a plan to land a man on the Moon. . . . Wow!"[12] It seemed more and more likely that regular people, not just astronauts, would be able to experience space travel one day. Rutan longed to be one of those people when the time came.

By the early 1990s, however, Rutan's excitement had turned into disappointment. NASA and other space agencies were not moving as quickly as Rutan thought they should. "I realized that waiting for NASA wasn't going to work," he says. "If my dream was going to come true—of floating weightless in the black sky and being thrilled by the sight of Earth from outside our atmosphere—I'd have to get things started myself." [13]

Eyes on the Prize

In his usual manner, Rutan started making sketches on stray napkins, and before long his head was full of ideas for spacecraft. In 1996, he shared some of these ideas with a space enthusiast named Paul Allen. Allen was fascinated by the things Rutan had to say. As the cofounder of Microsoft, he was also one of the richest men in the world. He had plenty of money to finance Rutan's dreams if the right project could be found.

Several months later, the perfect opportunity appeared. A businessman named Peter Diamandis announced that he would give $10 million to the first nongovernment team to create a working spacecraft. To win the award, which was called the X Prize, the craft had to do several things. It had to travel higher than 62 miles (100km); it had to carry a human pilot plus the weight of two other people; and it had to do this twice within a two-week period. Diamandis required two trips because his goal was to encourage space tourism. The second trip would prove that the spacecraft could be used more than once—an important feature for a vehicle that was supposed to make money one day.

Like everyone else in the aviation business, Rutan and Allen were intrigued by the X Prize. They were not sure the money would actually appear, but they found the challenge more interesting than the cash anyway. The two men agreed to pursue the prize together. Rutan would be the creative end of the partnership, and Allen would provide $25 million in funding.

Rutan was unusually nervous about this venture. "It was extremely risky technology," he admits today. "We were a company that had never built a **supersonic** aircraft, and here we had to go straight up into space at [three times the speed of sound]."[14] Still, Rutan was excited, and he got right to work on his new project. Over the next few years, a vehicle called *SpaceShipOne* took shape inside the hangars of Scaled Composites. The finished spacecraft used Scaled's unique composite construction. It had delta wings, two tail fins, and a cabin just large enough to carry three people.

The craft's most original feature was something Rutan called a shuttlecock system. A shuttlecock is a feathered ball that is used in the sport of badminton. Because of its shape, a shuttlecock automatically tips into a certain position when it starts to fall. By designing *SpaceShipOne* to do the same thing, Rutan hoped to make it safer and easier for the vehicle to return to the ground.

A Great Success

Rutan started testing *SpaceShipOne* in May 2003. Over the next year, the spacecraft flew fifteen times. Its performance got better and better as problems were found and fixed. On the last test flight, *SpaceShipOne* rose just above the 62-mile-high (100km) border between air and space. The vehicle was officially a spacecraft, and its pilot, Mike Melvill, was history's first civilian astronaut.

At this point, *SpaceShipOne* was ready to compete for the X Prize (which was now officially called the Ansari X Prize). Rutan contacted prize officials and set a date of September 29, 2004, for the first flight. With pilot Melvill at the controls once again, the

Space Is Fun

Burt Rutan says he did not intend to change the world when he built *SpaceShipOne*. He did it because the project was challenging and fun. In this respect, he feels that he has a lot in common with earlier aviation pioneers. He describes this connection with these words:

> Five years after the Wright brothers' first flight, in 1903, the airplane was still just a dangerous curiosity. Only a dozen or so people had ventured into the air. Yet by 1912 hundreds of pilots had flown a number of different designs developed around the world, with crashes weeding out the bad ideas. Soon factories in France, England, and Germany were producing hundreds, and then thousands, of airplanes a year. Why? I believe the answer lay in two observations: "That's gotta be fun" and "Maybe I can do that." Clearly, if private spaceships were going to be built, they would also need to be created for fun by those discovering that "maybe I can do that."

—Burt Rutan, "Rocket for the Rest of Us," *National Geographic*, April 2005, p. 31.

SpaceShipOne, **designed and built by Burt Rutan, lands safely in the Mojave Desert after its historic flight.**

small craft was carried upward by a Rutan airplane called the White Knight. It was released at an altitude of about 9 miles (14.5km). *SpaceShipOne* then fired a rocket engine and blasted upward at a top speed of more than 2,000 miles per hour (3,218kph). It eventually reached a height of about 64 miles (103km) before starting its downward journey. The spacecraft's first X Prize flight was a success.

Following its successful flight, Burt Rutan (left) and Paul Allen donated *SpaceShipOne* to the National Air and Space Museum.

SpaceShipOne's second flight occurred on October 4, 2004. Flown this time by Brian Binnie, the little vehicle rocketed nearly 70 miles (112km) into the sky before returning safely to Earth. At the end of the flight, Rutan and all of Scaled's employees were ecstatic. Not only had they just won the X Prize, they had changed the field of space travel as well. Officials at the Smithsonian immediately understood this fact and got Rutan's permission to display *SpaceShipOne* in the National Air and Space Museum.

Asked at the time if he thought his accomplishment was historic, Rutan answered,

> I think it's undeniable. I think we've proven now that the small guys can build a spaceship and go to space. . . . I will predict that in 12 or 15 years, there will be tens of thousands, maybe even hundreds of thousands, of people that fly and see that black sky. And in 10 to 12 years, kids will not just hope, but they will know that they can go to orbit in their lifetimes. [15]

Next Steps

Rutan's words show where his interests lie. Although $10 million is a lot of money, Rutan was never motivated by the X Prize cash. He built *SpaceShipOne* because it was fun and he wanted to achieve his life-long dream of going to space. Rutan has

A Driven Life

Burt Rutan's work-obsessed lifestyle has taken a toll on his personal life. The designer is currently married to his fourth wife, Tonya, after going through three divorces. Work has affected Rutan's health as well. He had a heart attack in 1998. As a result of his heart problems, Rutan has cut down on his work hours. He says he now works 60 or 70 hours a week instead of 100 or more, as he used to do.

Health issues have not stopped Rutan from being creative. In his spare time, he has designed many nonflying objects, including golf putters and even his own house. The odd-looking house is shaped like several pyramids and is dug into a hillside.

In spite of health problems, Burt Rutan continues to work as many as 70 hours a week.

**Tethered under its launch plane the White Knight, *SpaceShipOne*
takes its first flight during Rutan's successful quest for the X Prize.**

not yet made the journey himself, but he fully intends to go
someday—and he plans to help thousands of other people to
make the trip as well. In 2004 he said:

> I think I will spend a large percentage, if not all, of my
> main efforts for the rest of my career on manned–space
> travel. I think we can be . . . within 20 to 25 years of be-
> ing able to visit hotels in orbit and many thousands of
> people being able to afford to do that. I would [also] like
> to see affordable travel to the moon before I die.[16]

To make these things happen, Rutan is working with a major
company called Virgin Galactic. (Virgin Galactic is part of the Virgin

Group, the same organization that sponsored *GlobalFlyer*.) Rutan is currently designing and building a fleet of spacecraft for Virgin. The first public flights may blast off as soon as the year 2008 if all goes well. At more than $200,000 per ticket, these early flights will be expensive. Rutan expects the price to fall quickly. Soon, he says, "at a very affordable price, something like you'd spend for a luxury cruise vacation, you can be an astronaut."[17]

There is no doubt that Rutan's dreams are big. Many people say they are too big—that Rutan will never be able to do the things he is planning. But this innovator has proved over and over that he knows how to make seemingly impossible things happen. If Rutan reaches his current goals, he will be remembered forever as a space pioneer along with his many other remarkable achievements.

NOTES

Chapter 1: Fascinated by Flight

1. Quoted in Diane Tedeschi, "Talking with Burt Rutan, Aircraft Designer," *Air & Space Online,* August 14, 2002. www.airand spacemagazine.com/ASM/Web/TWD/Rutan.html.
2. Quoted in Joe Godfrey, "Elbert L. 'Burt' Rutan," Allstar Network, February 3, 2000. www.allstar.fiu.edu/aero/rutan2.htm.
3. Quoted in Alec Wilkinson, "Extraterrestrials: The Flying Rutan Brothers of Mojave, California, Long Ago Loosed the Surly Bonds of Earth, and the Ground Just Hasn't Felt Like Home Since Then," *Esquire,* June 1998, p. 86.
4. Quoted in Godfrey, "Elbert L. 'Burt' Rutan."
5. Quoted in Tedeschi, "Talking with Burt Rutan, Aircraft Designer."

Chapter 2: Building a Reputation

6. Quoted in Jim Schefter, "Wild Wings Reshape the Way We Fly," *Popular Science,* February 1990, p. 59.
7. Quoted in Tim Stevens, "Just Plane Smart," *Industry Week,* December 15, 1997, p. 94.
8. Quoted in Schefter, "Wild Wings Reshape the Way We Fly," p. 60.

Chapter 3: Imagination and Innovation

9. Quoted in Wilkinson, "Extraterrestrials," p. 91.
10. Quoted in Tedeschi, "Talking with Burt Rutan, Aircraft Designer."

11. Quoted in Tedeschi, "Talking with Burt Rutan, Aircraft Designer."

Chapter 4: To Space . . . and Beyond

12. Quoted in Leonard David, "Burt Rutan: Building 'Tomorrowland' One Launch at a Time," Space.com, October 14, 2004. www.space.com/news/rutan_interview_041014.html.

13. Burt Rutan, "Rocket for the Rest of Us," *National Geographic,* April 2005, p. 32.

14. Quoted in David H. Freedman, "Burt Rutan, Entrepreneur of the Year," *Inc.,* January 2005, p. 63.

15. Quoted on *60 Minutes,* CBS, November 7, 2004.

16. Quoted in George Nemiroff, "*SpaceShipOne* Designer Talks About Flight's Future," The Space Fellowship, December 21, 2004. www.spacefellowship.com/News/index.php?p=678.

17. Quoted in Bruce V. Bigelow, "Engineer Sees Opportunity for Civilian Spaceflight," *Free Republic,* June 14, 2004. www.free republic.com/focus/f-news/1153225/posts.

GLOSSARY

aerodynamics: A science that deals with the motion of air and other gases and with the forces acting on bodies exposed to them

aeronautical engineering: Using science and math to solve flight problems and build airplanes.

aeronautics: The science that deals with the operation of aircraft.

altitude: Distance above sea level.

aviation: Having to do with designing, building, and flying aircraft.

canard: A pair of nose-mounted wings on an airplane.

composite construction: A method of building airplanes that uses shaped foam and fiberglass instead of metal for the body, wings, and other major parts.

delta wings: Wings that, seen together, form the shape of a triangle.

entrepreneur: A person who dreams up, creates, and manages a business rather than working for someone else.

home builders: In the aviation industry, hobbyists who build their own airplanes at home.

homebuilts: Airplanes that have been built by a hobbyist.

innovators: People who come up with original ideas or do old things in a new way.

prototype: A one-of-a-kind, working model of an airplane. Prototypes are used to find and work out problems before full-size airplanes are built.

stalling: Losing lift during flight.

supersonic: Faster than the speed of sound.

wind tunnel: A design tool that lets scientists blast air at a full-size or model airplane. The scientists then study the airflow to spot possible flight problems.

FOR FURTHER EXPLORATION

Books

Caroline Bingham, *DK Big Book of Airplanes*. New York: Dorling Kindersley, 2001. This fact-packed picture book includes plenty of photos and diagrams. Informative text, scattered throughout the book, provides basic facts along with some airplane trivia.

Careers in Focus: Aviation. New York: Facts On File, 2005. This book for young adults talks about airplane-related jobs.

Ole Steen Hansen, *The B-2 Spirit Stealth Bomber*. Mankato, MN: Capstone, 2006. Learn about the "stealth" bomber that Burt Rutan helped to test.

Andrew Haslam, *Make It Work! Science: Flight*. Chicago: Two-Can, 2000. This book discusses the science of airplane flight, then shows how to build gadgets to demonstrate this science in action.

Tamra Orr, *The Dawn of Aviation: The Story of the Wright Brothers*. Hockessin, DE: Mitchell Lane, 2005. This book tells the story of two early aviation pioneers who changed the world.

Judith E. Rinard, *The Story of Flight*. Buffalo, NY: Firefly, 2002. Produced in cooperation with the Smithsonian National Air and Space Museum, this book reviews the history of flight.

Tom Sibila, *SpaceShipOne: Making Dreams Come True*. Bloomington, MN: Red Brick Learning, 2006. An in-depth look at the story and background of Burt Rutan's *SpaceShipOne*, the first privately funded craft to reach outer space.

Web Sites

Air & Space Online (www.airandspacemagazine.com/ASM/Web/ TWD/Rutan.html). This Web site includes a 2002 interview with Burt Rutan.

Scaled Composites (www.scaled.com). This is the Web site of Scaled Composites. Highlights projects Burt Rutan and his team are working on today.

Smithsonian National Air and Space Museum (www.nasm. si.edu). This Web site shows the National Air and Space Museum's collections, exhibitions, research, and more.

Virgin Atlantic GlobalFlyer (www.virginatlanticglobal flyer.com). This Web site provides up-to-the-minute reports on *GlobalFlyer's* activities. It includes great photos, quizzes, games, and much more.

INDEX

PICTURE CREDITS

ABOUT THE AUTHOR

Kris Hirschmann has written more than 100 books for children. She owns and runs the Wordshop (www.the-wordshop.com), a business that provides a variety of writing and editorial services. She holds a bachelor's degree in psychology from Dartmouth College in Hanover, New Hampshire.

Hirschmann lives just outside Orlando, Florida, with her husband, Michael, and her daughters, Nikki and Erika.